THE
EUCHARISTIC PRAYER

THE
EUCHARISTIC PRAYER

by

J. A. JUNGMANN, S. J.

Translated by Robert L. Batley

1956
CHALLONER PUBLICATIONS
LONDON

First published in German under the
title of *Das Eucharistiche Hochgebet*
by Werkbund-Verlag

First published in English in 1956

Nihil Obstat: Dermitus Fogarty, S.T.D.
                Censor Deputatus

Imprimatur: H. Gibney
                Vicarius Generalis

Datum Southwarci, die 13a Februarii 1956

Printed in Great Britain by
J. Cook & Son (Printers) Ltd., Lower Ashley Road, Bristol 2

FOREWORD TO THE GERMAN EDITION

by HEINRICH KAHLEFELD

THE series which begins with this present book requires a word of introduction. Ever since 1948 in the castle of Rothenfels near Mainz, the practice of the 1930's was renewed of holding study-weeks for the younger generation as well as professional conferences. Church architects, politicians, physicists, artists, teachers, pastors and doctors in turn each devoted a week every year to the study of the theology of scripture and the liturgy.

The matter dealt with in the series of lectures has been preserved in chapter form. The participants of these study weeks desire to gain, under the guidance of a duly qualified teacher, not a technical knowledge, but a knowledge of their chosen subject which makes possible honest and well-founded judgments.

It would seem that the lecture is best suited to the type of person who frequents these study weeks, for a lecture can only contain an introduction with a certain development of one specific question, with perhaps a general survey of the whole subject. Its purpose is to encourage and enable such a person to continue studying the matter in greater detail later on. Such a method is greatly hampered, the more so because a study week can scarcely last longer than five or six days. But perhaps this is an advantage in that it makes a genuine introduction possible.

The purpose of this series is to enable a greater number to share in the wealth of material contained in these study weeks by putting into their hands a reliable document of the proceedings.

The four chapters contained in this present volume are the

four lectures given by Professor Josef A. Jungmann SJ at the Liturgical Week for priests at Rothenfels in 1952 and repeated in January 1953 at a liturgical conference for 500 priests from West Berlin and the East Zone of Germany.

We are publishing these lectures at the express wish of the participants and of many others, although they are a mere reflection of Professor Jungmann's great work in two volumes *Missarum Solemnia*,[1] and the first lecture of this present book is much in line with his previous one entitled 'The Memorial of the Lord in the Eucharistia', also published in the *Theologische Quartalschrift* 133 (1953) pp. 385 *seq*.

We feel that precisely because in the present form the lines of Professor Jungmann's thought are more clearly marked and set out with the interests of parish-priests in mind, it will be possible for the reader to tackle his more important works with greater ease.

[1] *Missarum Solemnia* has been translated into English in America under the title of 'The Mass of the Roman Rite'.

CONTENTS

CHAPTER I

MEMORES

SOME of you no doubt will be surprised that I have chosen a few simple words from the Canon of the Mass as the subject of my lectures, words whose meaning is clear to everyone and which appear to require no further explanation. But it is quite clear that these words are fundamental, of very ancient standing and contain in a nutshell the whole of the Mass-liturgy. And this after all is their intention. I am going to try and show how the rest of the liturgy of the Mass has developed with all its various forms from a few fundamental ideas, present in Revelation and the Last Supper, ideas which were manifest in the liturgy of the early Christians.

Often these words can only be understood when they are interpreted historically; in other words we must attempt to understand the original meaning at the time when they were introduced into the liturgy.

We will begin with the word *Memores*, a short word, which only seems to possess any importance because of its proximity to the heart of the Mass. *Memores*: remembering Thy Sacred Passion, Thy Resurrection from the dead and Thy glorious Ascension. This is what is called the Anamnesis. The word 'Unde' links it up with the Institution of the Blessed Sacrament, with the sacramental word itself. On the other hand it seems to be nothing more than an amplification of the real meaning which is contained in this prayer after the consecration in the words: *offerimus praeclarae maiestati tuae*. The same prayer is used in the oriental liturgy μεμνημενοι προτφερομεν. But the Armenian liturgy reverses the relationship. 'Remembering' becomes the dominant and fundamental expression, while 'offering' is subordinated to it; insofar as we offer, we remember.

Obviously this word *Memores* cannot then be dealt with

I

superficially. It is fundamental to the meaning of the Mass; in fact this memorial character has an equal importance with the sacrificial character.

We have only to glance through the articles on the Mass by many authors in the *Dictionnaire de Théologie Catholique* to realise that these two ideas dominate everything else: the Mass as memorial and the Mass as sacrifice. Authors of an older period who wrote on the Eucharist and the Mass in homilies and letters did not bother themselves very much with a systematic marshalling of their ideas, but their writings obviously embrace these two fundamental ideas, remembrance and sacrifice.

But since the Council of Trent, since the Reformation when the sacrificial character of the Mass was being denied, the balance between these two ideas is no longer so common. The effect of this controversy was to focus all attention on the idea of sacrifice; even theologians went so far as to attempt to sum up the whole doctrine of the Mass in this one idea of sacrifice. They tried to do this by speaking of the relative sacrifice. The sacrifice of the Mass refers back to the sacrifice on the Cross. It is at the same time a remembrance of the sacrifice on the Cross, because according to the words of Trent there is the same sacrificial gift and the same offerer.

The idea of remembrance, therefore, is still present in the exposition now usual. But it is to some extent confined to that moment in the history of redemption, which we understand by the idea of sacrifice: the self-giving to God the Father, in suffering and death. Of course we can define the idea of sacrifice in another way, so that it goes a step further and embraces its visible acceptance by God the Father in the resurrection and triumph of Christ. But we have to admit that our habitual grasp of the commemorative nature of the Mass is rather weak; it is certainly not so live and fresh as in the case of its sacrificial aspect.

It is important, therefore, to consider carefully the full content of this idea of the Mass as a memorial of the Lord; all the more so because, in the liturgy of the Mass as we actually have it, various elements only really become intelligible when we try and understand them with the help of the idea of remembrance. Let us be clear about this: the remembrance of the facts of the redemption is essential and fundamental for Christianity. This is what distinguishes Christianity from all natural religions, be they pantheistic, polytheistic or monotheistic. These religions as well as the Greek mystery-religions expressed their worship by representing the unchanging events of nature, embodied in a symbolical form. They were concerned only with the eternal return of spring and autumn, of flowering and withering, and they attempted to influence favourably these events of nature by magical powers and make them subservient to them. But these religions remained and still remain in the natural sphere. Christianity is entirely an historical religion. It builds upon this one historical fact which goes beyond nature, that Jesus Christ, the Son of God, came into this world and redeemed us. This He did at a definite point in time and space. The thinking back to this fact, the constant looking and referring back, is therefore essential. This referring back takes place in two ways: by means of sacred signs, sacramentally, so that the past act of redemption becomes effective for us; secondly through the psychological reflection and calling to mind by the Christian people, because it should be an intelligent drawing on the source of salvation opened up for us; it should be a personal relationship with God.

These statements are all the more important the more one relies on the ancient mystery-religions for throwing light on Christian ceremonies. For in some of them we find instances of redemptive acts; in others also the idea of participation in the fruits of redemption, and that by means of established rites. But then we come up against the fundamental difference: on the one hand are happenings on the mere plane of nature, while on the other is the fact that, in the fullness of time, God Himself entered this world at a definite historical moment—the Word was made flesh and redeemed us by dying upon the Cross.

If we are to understand the meaning of 'remembrance' in its true light, we must consider something else. Within Christianity and within the Church we find constantly this inclination towards bringing into religion what is purely natural, an inclination which from time to time assumes acute forms. Think of recent discoveries in modern Protestantism and think of the idea of 'positive Christianity'. Even within the Church there was the period of rationalism, when many people thought of Christianity simply as a means of devotion, as a support for morality and virtue, when the only idea of Christ which remained was that of a great friend of mankind. What belonged to the natural order of creation received an undue and excessive importance. This extended to the performance of religious ceremonies. Think of the Credo in the Mass by Franz Schubert, where for all practical purposes one never gets beyond the acknowledgment of creation: 'Noch lag die Schöpfung formlos da (Still lies creation shapeless there)'. Or just think of most of the modern catechisms where the doctrine of grace and the sacraments follows immediately after the main chapter on the commandments, strictly orthodox and correct concerning individual points. But the resulting effect is that it helps the impression that we need grace only so that we may keep the commandments; first let us have the commandments, then sanctifying grace. Grace and Christianity in the minds of children and the faithful, who do not understand the finer points of theology, are brought down to this level: they are necessary to help us do what is morally and naturally the right thing.

It is, however, of the greatest importance that we understand Christianity as an historical religion, not only in the sphere of theology, but in the entire pastoral field. Christ as the Son of God and the Son of man; the beginning of the New Race; His work of redemption on the Cross, the source of salvation; without Him and therefore without the Church there is no possibility of salvation, but in Him there is light and life and the aristocracy of the children of God.

I believe that this is the only way to make the faithful conscious of the character of Christianity as a supernatural religion, a religion which goes beyond the order of nature; the way is through the Anamnesis. Otherwise we may define the idea of grace as exactly as we like, illustrate it with the most beautiful pictures, compare it to a marriage garment, to the light of the soul, and in the end not very much of it will remain.

It seems we have rather strayed from our liturgical theme and are now involved in a fundamental discussion on how to teach the faith. But at the same time we have found a basis for a more complete appreciation of the *Unde et memores* and of other forms which may be drawn from it. The *memoria* therefore is really present in the liturgy of the Mass, and it is fixed in the principal place of the liturgy, as the first word after the words of consecration. It is placed there with a breadth of perspective to which we must pay special attention. Not only is the sacrifice on the Cross (understood as strictly as you like) mentioned, but after the *beata passio*, the resurrection and the glorification follow immediately. *Necnon et ab inferis resurrectionis sed et in caelos gloriosae ascensionis.*

The whole work of salvation is described with a few strokes of the pen. Not only is the death on the Cross mentioned, in which we recognise theologically the decisive act of redemption, the proper *causa efficiens meritoria* of the redemption, but both the resurrection and the ascension are included as well, the *causa exemplaris* of the redemption, the prototype of redeemed man, which is made visible and becomes evident in the risen and glorified Christ.

Perhaps I may express myself in another way: according to the way of speaking among the early Christians, the work of redemption was expressed in picture form by a battle—Christ in the battle of freedom for mankind. But this pictorial expression could not remain where it was in apparent defeat in Christ's passion and death. The turning point of the redemptive drama had to be included as well: the victory of the resurrection and the ascension to His throne of the *kyrios*. Heinz Schürmann has published a small book on this subject, *The basis and structure of New Testament Preaching* (Paderborn, 1949). There he points out how the preaching of the apostles was concerned first and foremost with these basic facts of our religion.

Our Lord's injunction, as far as the content of remembrance is concerned, reads rather vaguely: 'Do this in memory of Me'. 'In memory of Me'—implying, 'you ought to know yourselves what I am to you and what you have to thank Me for'. St Paul says more exactly: 'As often as ye shall do this, ye shall show forth the Death of the Lord'. But we know what St

Paul meant by the 'Death of the Lord'; the idea of Christ's triumph was for him inseparably linked up with the idea of death. The oldest mass-formula, which Hippolytus of Rome wrote in Greek (c. 215), reads: *memores igitur mortis et resurrectionis eius*. The text of our present Roman Canon offers therefore the legitimate and final development of what was intended from the beginning. Final of course only in a limited sense: here is laid down in a brief juridical form what occurs objectively during the whole sacramental act: *memores offerimus*, remembrance and sacrifice.

The subjective memory of the Church and, to a certain extent, what we may call the resonance of the sacramental act in the consciousness of the Church (by Church I mean the minds of the faithful worshipping together), needs greater latitude. This is in fact given to 'remembrance' in our Mass liturgy, and is done in two ways: in the Thanksgiving-prayer and in the Scripture readings.

The liturgy of the Mass as we know it from early times (at least since the second century) has always been considered as a great prayer of thanksgiving, as *Eucharistia*. Even today we begin, after various preparations, the real Actio with the cry: *gratias agamus*. The idea of a thanksgiving-prayer, of *Eucharistia*, has grown up so closely with the sacramental act of the Mass, that even today we speak of the sacrament as the Eucharist.

Thanksgiving and remembering are very closely connected. If we look at the content of thanksgiving, it is seen to be nothing else but 'thinking of'. To think of that which has been received, to express it and show it; to recognise and acknowledge it, to show by acknowledgment at least in words, and perhaps with more than words. The meaning of the thanksgiving-prayer is essentially this: in prayer before God we call to mind what we have received, and what the basis of our hope is: the great outlines of the work of redemption and the history of redemption, climaxing in the death and resurrection of Christ.

In the oldest text of the Mass liturgy by Hippolytus of Rome which is extant, this theme is expressed with splendid clarity: *Gratias tibi referimus, per dilectum puerum tuum Jesum Christum, quem in ultimis temporibus misisti nobis salvatorem et redemptorem et angelum voluntatis tuae. Qui est Verbum tuum inseparabile, per quem omnia fecisti et bene placitum tibi fuit. Misisti de caelo in matricem Virginis; qui (que) in utero habitus incarnatus est et Filius tibi ostensus est ex Spiritu Sancto et Virgine natus. Qui voluntatem tuam complens et populum sanctum tibi adquirens extendit manus cum pateretur, ut a passione liberaret eos qui in te crediderunt. Qui cum (que) traderetur voluntariae passioni ut mortem solvat et vincula diaboli dirumpat et infernum calcet et iustos inluminet et terminum figat et resurrectionem manifestet, accipiens panem gratias tibi agens dixit: Accipite, manducate. . . .*

The whole section before the consecration is therefore considered as a single, thanking remembrance. Perhaps it has also struck you that there is a great similarity between this prayer of thanksgiving or remembrance and the Apostolic creed. This is easy to understand because the content is in both cases the same.

In the prayer of thanksgiving there is first the reference to God the Father; then the work of redemption is described—the coming of the Son of God into the world, into a virgin's womb; then the struggle of the passion and the triumph of the resurrection, made effective for us, for His Church. In the creed these main points remain the same: God the Almighty Father; Christ conceived of the Holy Spirit, born of a Virgin; the passion, the triumph of the resurrection, and finally the Church and the salvation to be found therein.

In the creed the mode of expression is simpler, more positive and more to the point, because they are statements, essential declarations, of what a Christian believes. In the Thanksgiving-prayer the style is on a higher plane, more solemn, even lyrical, because it is a speech of thanks to One whom we cannot but thank for His grace and mercy *semper et ubique*. For this reason the thanksgiving-prayer of the Mass was called simply 'confession' (ἐξομολόγησις in the Greek; *contestatio* in the Gallic liturgy). Conversely the creed was known as *Eucharistia*. In the Roman liturgy a name which emphasised the solemnity of the thanksgiving-prayer became common: *praefatio*. Today many prayer books, manuals of devotion and even books on liturgy translate the word '*praefatio*' by 'preface'. That is to say the least a misleading translation. Of course the word may be translated literally as 'preface', but this must not be understood in the sense of an introduction. *Praefatio* means a 'speech before something'. But that 'before' must not be understood as refering to time, but to space; as prayer and speech before God and before the community of the faithful. A good translation of the word is GREAT PRAYER. By GREAT PRAYER we usually understand the whole of the Eucharistic Prayer from *gratias agamus* to the *Pater noster*; but originally this was what *Praefatio* stood for as well. At any rate we must view the whole of the GREAT PRAYER from *gratias agamus* to the *Pater noster* as a unity, where at least in the first half, the dominant idea is thanksgiving, passing easily over to the mood of worship and offering.

Now in the present form of the Roman Mass the Preface, with its pervading mood of thanksgiving, has been cut off from what follows, from the Canon in the strict sense. The Preface is said out loud, even sung; the Canon in the strict sense is only read (since the ninth century it has been said in a low voice, to point to the Mystery which is being accomplished). But as far as its content goes, the Preface has lost a good deal, if we care to look merely at the wording. This is particularly true of the Common Preface. It is also true of the Preface of the Apostles and of the Blessed Trinity, which is said on Sundays. There we do not feel much of the ancient theme of thanksgiving for the Work of Redemption. But the ancient theme is to be found more clearly in our Prefaces for feast days and festive seasons. But the theme is split up into the various stages in which the work of redemption was carried out. If we put all these festive prefaces together, we have a perfect *Eucharistia* in the old style: giving thanks that Mary bore the Son of God in the undiminished splendour of her Virginity; that in Him a new light has shone forth upon us; that God wrought our salvation on the wood of the Cross; that Christ conquered death by dying and by His resurrection won back life; that He allowed His heart to be pierced to create for us a haven of salvation; that He ascended into Heaven to grant us a share in His divinity; that He has poured out upon us the spirit of adoption.

In the old Roman liturgy before Gregory the Great, there existed a great number of Prefaces of this kind; in fact it became a principle that every feast and every Mass had to have its own Preface. But this was a dangerous principle. For example, if every feast of a saint or martyr had to have its own Preface, one ran the risk of removing the main theme from the centre of the picture and allowing it to remain in the background. Individual points became quite sufficient and a picture would be drawn of the sufferings of a martyr; the prayer of thanksgiving became a petition, as has happened to some extent with the Preface of the Apostles; or a creed, as has happened in the case of the Preface of the Blessed Trinity.

This led to a sharp reaction. Towards the end of the sixth century the majority of such Prefaces had been abandoned. In the end only nine or ten Prefaces were left, and our Common Preface, which previously had never been considered as an independent Preface but rather as a framework for various special Prefaces, became the normal form of our thanksgiving prayer.

That was certainly to be prefered to the unrestrained growth of Prefaces in the sixth century, although now we must hasten to admit that instead of excess a certain poverty exists. We feel this especially on Sundays, in the Community-Mass, when a lector reads out to the faithful the Preface of the Blessed Trinity, which in any case does not come from the early Roman tradition. What we would like to hear is the joy of the resurrection being expressed on Sundays, the day when our redemption was completed, and the rejoicings of the redeemed becoming meaningful once again. In former times there was a great number of such Prefaces; let us hope that some of them will return.

We feel the poverty of our Thanksgiving-prayer especially in the Common Preface. Nevertheless, it does possess a certain grandeur, and there is a nobility in the simplicity of this Preface. To a degree it presumes that the Christian knows for what he has to give thanks; that he experiences in his own consciousness the divine benefits, benefits of the natural order, and above all those which concern the order of salvation. Only one thing is mentioned: we must thank Him always and everywhere, *semper et ubique*; we must thank Him and ought to thank Him through Christ our Lord. With this *per Christum Dominum nostrum*, the all important word has been spoken. Only one word is necessary to express what is greatest. Christ has been sent down to us; through Him God's grace has come down to us; in Him the enormous chasm has been bridged, which separates fallen man from His God; in Him and through Him our prayer of thanksgiving shall rise up to God the Father. This *per Christum* occurs again in another form. The Common Preface continues: *per quem maiestatem tuam laudant angeli*. These words open up a glimpse of the angelic choirs and of their eternal praise of the Creator. It states that the angelic choirs are gathered about Him praising Him through Christ (*per quem*); that He is therefore in His glorified humanity the King who embraces heaven and earth.

So the Common Preface fulfills literally, what without further analysis and distinction, is contained in Our Lord's injunction: 'Do this in memory of Me'.

Such simplicity of language, which we find to its fullest extent in the Common Preface and to a degree in the feast day Prefaces, is possible when we remember that the memorial of the Lord and His work of salvation is expressed in a second (or third) form in the Scripture readings.

Let us straightway point out that the Christian Thanksgiving-prayer refers back finally to that prayer of thanksgiving which at the time of Christ was customary after almost every festive meal; thanks were given not only for the food received but for all the benefits which God had shown to His people. In the same way it can be proved that the Service of Reading is a continuation of that service of scripture reading which took place in the synagogues on the Sabbath. With certain clues we may say that there is a pretty close connection. But we must put the question: why did Christian consciousness make use of and preserve this pre-Christian order and develop it still further? This was the case with the Thanksgiving-prayer, because throughout Christendom in face of the greatness of Divine mercy, gratitude became first and foremost a necessity and foundation of Christian prayer. Similarly with the Scripture readings, because it was worth keeping always in mind the *magnalia Dei*, and the exhortations and teachings which God had linked up with them. In both cases the historical character of Christianity and the memorial character of Christian worship form the background. So the Service of Reading stands to a certain extent as a second, broader sounding-board from which the sacramental act of the Lord's memorial may echo.

We must also add that in the case of these readings, even where they are historical passages, it is not merely a question of remembering historical events. Of course the exhortations from one of the Apostle's epistles are to be reckoned as directed to the congregation which is assembled. But even the Gospel account of events in the life of Christ is more than a mere historical account. And I am not thinking of a certain event becoming actually present again in its historical reality. For example, Christ once healed the sick and that still occurs today; it occurs in the giving of the Sacraments, in Penance, in Extreme Unction; Christ once stilled the storm at sea; that still occurs inasmuch as the Christ-Mystery, in God's good time, will still the troubled times of today.

But the idea with which the readings are concerned can, to a greater or less extent, be made effective: that is, in the making present of the historical and ever-present work of redemption in the Church and in the hearts of the faithful.

The world of Faith must take shape again, if the Mystery of Faith is to become effective. This can and ought in effect to happen in such a way that the Word of God is preached to the faithful. I mean read to them in an intelligible manner: in their own language, therefore, and directed towards them, and then, if the occasion arises, developed and applied in the homily. There is also the way, at least as an outside possibility, that these readings occur under certain circumstances symbolically in the sacred Latin language, not in the form of a reading, but spoken in a low voice by the priest alone turned towards the altar. Such a reading cannot be called meaningless, at least provided that it does not become general (at present we have in the Community-Mass the possibility of a parallel reading in the vernacular) and provided that the symbolism at least means something.

That is at any rate the case when the dignity of our Gospel is in various ways made visible and prominent. This is especially true of High Mass: it is not any lector, but the deacon who sings it. Before the reading he takes his place in a small procession, preceded by acolytes and incense. A special place of honour is provided for the reading. The deacon does not hold the book himself, as the subdeacon does at the epistle, but it is held for him. Beforehand he seeks a special blessing. He begins with an announcement which precedes the greeting, which otherwise only occurs before the *Oratio* and before the Preface. Everyone stands. Christ is acknowledged as being really present in the Gospel. He is given a greeting: *Gloria Tibi, Domine*. Everyone makes the sign of the cross. The deacon sings the Gospel in a solemn tone, for it is after all the Good News! At the conclusion of the Gospel the book is kissed in grateful reverence. A good part of the ceremonial privileges afforded to the Gospel have been preserved in the *Missa Cantata* and in the *Missa Lecta*; especially the place of honour; the server must at least carry the missal over from the epistle side. Historically speaking the place of honour is on the right hand of the Bishop, who had his *cathedra* at the top of the *apse*. The people of course do not understand the symbolism here, but, with a slightly different interpretation, it can become intelligible once more. It is the place of honour on the right hand side of the picture of Christ, on the right of the crucifix.

We cannot say that the people of the Middle Ages had a very deep understanding of the liturgy in general or of the Mass liturgy in particular. But the idea of *memoria* was certainly very much alive to them, much more so than the idea of sacrifice. The Mass as the *memoria passionis*, as the *memoria totius vitae Christi*, that was the chief idea with which people in the Middle Ages followed their Mass. Since the ninth century at least, the allegorical explanation of the Mass became the chief devotion during Mass. And it was not, especially at the beginning, a meaningless or arbitrary accumulation of relationships between the Mass and the Passion; rather was it an attempt to find in the course of the Mass the whole story of our salvation from the appeals of the Old

Testament Fathers in the *Kyrie*, right down to the blessing, given by our Lord to His disciples before His ascension, in the priest's Last Blessing. Whoever has read Calderon's *Mysteries of the Holy Mass*, will begin to understand the grandeur of this interpretation of the Mass. But this allegorizing is for us and for our people today, despite everything, no longer possible as the chief interpretation of the Mass. We are much more realistic, we want to see what is happening ourselves and we want to hear the words in our own tongue. But it is precisely the Anamnesis, the *Unde et memores*, which is the fundamental form of the actual liturgy of the Mass. But we must see it in its fullest extent, especially in the Thanksgiving-prayer and in the Scripture readings. Only then will we be fulfilling our Lord's command with fresh appreciation and renewed joy: 'Do this in memory of me.'

Chapter II

OFFERIMUS

WE have made the meaning and possible extent of the Anamnesis quite clear. Close to the Anamnesis there is placed with equal importance, usually more strongly emphasized in the Roman Mass, the sacrifice: *Unde et memores . . . offerimus praeclarae maiestati tuae*. The Mass is a Sacrifice. That has always been an article of faith. Even in the Didache the Mass was called θυσια; even then this almost solid, ancient word is used for sacrifice. And the same work sees the prophecy of Malachy concerning the pure sacrifice fulfilled in the Eucharist.

What is so striking is that the Mass appears in the liturgy at once and before all else as OUR sacrifice, and so it appears throughout: WE bring gifts, WE beg for acceptance, WE prepare MY sacrifice and YOUR sacrifice. On the other hand we are accustomed from the side of dogmatic theology to regard the Mass just as precisely and almost exclusively as the sacrifice of Christ. The fact that WE are offering is scarcely mentioned in theological discussions. The only topics discussed are the fact that Christ offers; enquiry is made as to how He offers, how He renews His sacrifice or makes it present, whether any destruction takes place or not. Even catechisms employ the same methods of consideration.

The Council of Trent was not, as a matter of fact, the first to declare the Mass as the sacrifice of Christ. You will find the same teaching among the Fathers, Chrysostom or Cyprian for example, who see the prototype of Melchisedech realised in the person of Christ. That is the constant tradition of the Catholic Church. Even the liturgies, including the Roman, express this quite clearly, perhaps not in words, but certainly in the rite in which the words of consecration are set. One can always point to the words 'This is my Body', which only means anything as the sacramental formula in the mouth of Christ or in the mouth of one who represents the person of Christ. But the words of themselves could perhaps be explained away, by saying that this is only an historical account. But we must consider the rite in its entirety. The rite makes it clear that the priest, when he begins the words of consecration, is no longer merely the representative of the assembled congregation, but that he represents now the person of Christ, because he does what Christ did. He takes bread in his hands, he takes the excellent chalice, *this* excellent chalice—implying that Christ takes this chalice. He blesses it and makes the sign of the cross over it (this is an expansion of the biblical text, certainly since the fifth century, but the will to do what Christ did reveals itself even here). Some liturgies go still further; at the word *fregit* the Host is broken, or a fraction is at least implied. This is also true of the oriental liturgies from the earliest times, or at least since the seventh century. (Individual gestures, e.g., the elevation of the Host and the Chalice are mentioned much earlier.) Only in the Byzantine liturgy does the priest omit any gestures of this kind, although this is an innovation as the result of controversy. The gestures in question were only abandoned when the Byzantine theologians rejected the theory that it was not the words of consecration but the epiclesis which completed the consecration.

The liturgy says both: the Mass is the Sacrifice of Christ, and: the Mass is OUR sacrifice, the sacrifice of the Church. The liturgy tells us that the Mass is the Sacrifice of Christ at the moment when it reaches its climax, when the inner Mystery must reveal itself. The liturgy tells us that the Mass is the sacrifice of the Church on a much wider scale throughout the course of the sacred actions. Indeed we can say: the sacrifice of Christ appears in the liturgy of the Holy Mass in a sense wrapped up in the sacrifice of the Church. It is important to take note of this because there are some who have called in question the correctness and propriety of saying at all that the Mass, though objectively Christ's sacrifice, displays externally any of the characteristics of a sacrifice or offering in the authentic and original sense of those words. Would it not be more correct to say that the basic form of the Mass is

exclusively the meal which is prepared and eaten! These
doubts arose because it seemed in some way improper to
represent what is most sacred so directly, especially when
the harsh idea of sacrifice and perhaps of the bloody enactment
were concerned.

We may, I think, make the following answer to these
doubts. The sacrifice of Christ is actually only hinted at; it
does not decide the basic shape of the Mass-liturgy; it is enclosed and enveloped by what touches us more closely, which
belongs to the sphere of our human life; in other words, the
sacrifice of the Church. What we see and hear is almost only
the sacrifice of the Church. We see the Church ascending the
Sacred Mount. On the summit of the mountain she receives
the sacrifice from the hands of her Master and offers it with
Him. The Church puts her hands in His Hands and offers His
Sacrifice together with Him; His Body and His Blood. We
see only the visible form of the Church and hear the prayers of
her lips. We hear the hymn with which she praises the sacrificial gift which is placed in her hands: *hostiam puram, hostiam
sanctam, hostiam immaculatam, panem sanctae vitae aeternae et
calicem salutis perpetuae.* But otherwise we see and hear only
what she herself does in the act of offering.

That the Mass is the sacrifice of Christ and of the Church
belongs to its innermost essence. Only midst the stress of
controversy could the idea of the sacrifice of the Church
become to a certain extent obscured, because one was forced
to defend the character of sacrifice at its most critical point, the
sacrifice of Christ. So, as occurs in all controversies, it was the
sacrifice of Christ which was almost entirely discussed with a
resultant onesidedness. But both go together. Our Lord made
His sacrifice alone on the cross, the sacrifice of the Old and
New Testaments, just as He prayed alone on the mountains of
Palestine. But now He no longer wishes to pray and offer
alone. Because it was the sacrifice of the New and Eternal
Testament, the people belonging to the New Testament
should have an opportunity of ratifying this sacrifice in all
places and at all times and they should have an opportunity of
making it their own. The redeemed of all peoples and all times
should be gathered together round this altar so that they may

be able to offer together with their Lord this great *sacrificium laudis*; so that they may join their voices and their actions in the great glorification of God which Our Lord began on the cross.

That is the meaning of the Mass as sacrifice. What we are concerned with here is not the fact that Christ's sacrifice can be enacted everywhere and time after time made actual for us; nor are we concerned with it being a source of grace which may avail all who are nearby, as though we had merely to hold ourselves in readiness to receive. The point at issue is that we are co-offerers with Christ, so that the one sacrifice which we offer with Him should be the expression not only of His, but also of our, obedient self-giving to God the Father. That is why what theologians say of every sacrifice must be true of this sacrifice in so far as it is our sacrifice also; namely, that it is *in genere signi*—it has real meaning only in so far as it expresses obedience and reverence for God existing in our hearts.

From this point the form of the offering prayers after the consecration becomes intelligible, and especially the phrasing of the second prayer of offering, the *Supra quae*. We have often been astonished and even objected to the fact that we human beings beg God to accept the sacrifice of His Son, and in so doing compare this incomparable Sacrifice with the sacrifices which Abel and Abraham and Melchisedech offered. That would of course be meaningless and lacking in reverence if it concerned only the sacrifice which Christ offers. But Christ's sacrifice is not concerned. His sacrifice has already been accepted, and accepted definitively. But it is the sacrifice which WE offer with Him here and now that is concerned, and we offer this sacrifice in a worthy manner only when we possess that inner conviction of mind of which this sacrifice is the sign, and when we possess at least as perfect an obedience, and an attitude of mind as full of surrender, as the patriarchs.

Only when this attitude of mind becomes effective in us, can we hope that God will accept our sacrifice in the favourable way in which he accepted the sacrifices of those holy men. If that is not the case, if perhaps there is no one at Mass who is interiorly prepared for it, if the priest himself celebrates unworthily, then it may well be that the harsh words of the prophet may be applied to the Most Holy Sacrifice: 'Your sacrifice is an abomination to me, because your hands are stained with blood and wickedness.' Naturally the ideal is quite different. Our attitude of mind must be much purer and on a higher plane than those of the great men of the Old Testament, because the sign of our sacrifice is much purer and more sublime. It is not any sign, not any gift of reverence which we offer to God, but the body and blood of Christ. Therefore Christ's attitude of mind must be our attitude of mind when we approach the altar of God, according to the exhortation of St Paul: 'Let this mind be in you, which was also in Christ Jesus.' (Phil. 2.5), and then he goes on to write about the complete emptying of self and the sacrifice of the Man-God. At least this idea stands before us as a challenge, as a high ideal; it is also expressed in the rite of the Mass in a single word, for the *offerimus* does not stand alone, but is joined and associated with the *memores*. This means that we can only offer in a fitting manner, when we do it with the consciousness that we are carrying out the work of Christ and that we are entering into His sacrifice and prayer. Only then is it a real and genuine sacrifice when beforehand we enter into the world of the principles and convictions with which He went to His death.

When however our sacrifice, the sacrifice of the Church, is mentioned in the liturgy, only a straightforward offering is intended, an *Offerre*, a carrying towards, just as one carries forward a gift of homage; there is no question of destruction or annihilation. But this carrying towards, this offering, is couched in impressive terms both before and after the consecration. It is expressed in a solemn prayer and the prayer is accompanied by the corresponding indicatory gesture. This is done every time the gifts, which we are to offer, are mentioned: *haec dona, haec munera . . . hostiam puram, hostiam sanctam. . . .* For the signs of the cross which accompany these words are only a stylized form of indication, a pointing towards, which quite naturally takes the form of a sign of the cross. Similarly in ancient religious manuscripts a small cross which emphasize the sacred character of the said text, often develops from the marks of punctuation.

Even before the consecration, 'offering' is mentioned in several places. If we disregard the Offertory, it occurs first in the *Te igitur*, where the petition is expressed for a favourable acceptance (which is only a more refined expression for the simple word 'offering'). The priest bows down every time just as one does in giving a gift to a royal or distinguished person. This offering even before the consecration is a characteristic of the Roman liturgy. Only the Egyptian liturgy shows similar features of long standing.

In the Canon of the Roman Mass the sacrifice which we offer is spoken of with a particular emphasis. Sacrifice indeed is more or less the chief idea in the inner province of the Canon. Here a question forces itself upon us: we have stated that the chief prayer of the Roman Mass has been designed as εὐχαριστία: as memorial and as thanksgiving. *Gratias agamus* is chanted aloud, and the whole Mass should be a *gratiarum actio*, and was so originally. How then does that agree with the fact that this idea of sacrifice is so widespread in the Mass? Surely two quite distinct ideas are linked together. Is it not so that the thanksgiving remains confined to a short *Praefatio*, Preface, and it is in actual fact the idea of sacrifice which reigns supreme? The question is not difficult to answer. There is no contradiction, and the old basic scheme is not denied. Certainly the emphasis in early times was placed on one aspect and later on another. The offering is the legitimate continuation of the Thanksgiving-prayer, only on a higher level. The Thanksgiving-prayer occurs first in words and expresses its interior attitude of mind. In what follows, the thanksgiving in words passes over to the thanksgiving of action, to what is done. The interior attitude of thanksgiving finds its expression now through the offering of a gift. If we wish to understand this more clearly, let us see what takes place in terms of everyday life. Someone wishes to honour a deserving personality by making him a presentation, let us say, of a golden ring or a diploma. First of all there is a speech of thanks or remembrance in which the man's merits are recalled and praised and afterwards he is given the gift of honour. In such a case there is probably little or no mention of the gift of honour, but of the man's merits. It is just the same with the

Canon of the Mass. First of all the speech of thanks, then the handing over of the gift, the sacrifice. This connection is also quite clearly expressed in the Canon of the Mass by a single word, by the word (*Te*) *igitur*. First the solemn prayer of thanksgiving, passing over to adoration which we offer in the Sanctus in company with the angelic choirs, and then the petition for the acceptance of our gift. In this sense, therefore, we pray Thee.

The two ideas 'thanksgiving' and 'sacrifice' are not really so foreign to one another within the framework of the Christian world of ideas as may at first sight appear. On the one side there is the chief objective of our thanking and remembering the sacrifice which Christ offered on the cross and with which He redeemed the world. And as far as this concerns an objective remembrance (not merely our psychological reflection, but a sacramental event), it must be conceded that with this remembrance the sacrifice of Christ is made present. But we arrive at the same conclusion if we begin with the idea of sacrifice. This shows that our sacrifice is linked up closely with the idea of the *Eucharistia*. Our sacrifice is not an enormous sacrifice like the sacrifices of the pagans and of the Old Testament, where regard was had to the quantity and market-value of the gifts and where the belief was that the divinity had to be appeased by hecatombs. Our sacrifice is a spiritual sacrifice. The material components almost disappear, they mean so little. Our sacrifice is worth something because it is the expression of a holy attitude of mind entirely given over to God, of the desire to give ourselves completely and the desire of Our High Priest Jesus Christ to give Himself completely.

Our sacrifice is utterly *sacrificium laudis*; it is completely thanksgiving and the praise of God; it is an *oblatio rationabilis*. This phrase *oblatio rationabilis* occurs in so many words in the Canon of the Mass: *Quam oblationem tu Deus . . . rationabilem acceptabilemque facere digneris*. 'May God bless our sacrificial gift, may He consecrate, render it valid and spiritual and so worthy of Him.' A great number of works have been published in recent years about the word '*rationabilis*'. Their authors have suggested that '*rationabilis*' means spiritual, as distinct from material, and what is external. They also point

out that at the time when this word was introduced into the
Canon its meaning had already weakened; it meant merely
correct, reasonable. I have kept to this interpretation myself in
the first and second editions of *Missarum Solemnia*. Meanwhile
the opinion was submitted, and it appears in the third edition,
that in the Canon this word must possess its original meaning
of 'spiritual', with the justification that words in sacred speech
often retain their older meaning, while in everyday speech
their meaning has already altered. Our sacrifice is a spiritual
sacrifice, and as such proceeds not only from the prayer of
thanksgiving but is itself almost entirely thanksgiving and
homage before God.

Nevertheless it is true that the spirituality of the Christian
sacrifice has not always been given the same emphasis. Later on
this emphasis began to weaken, and with it a certain contrast
(I do not say a tension) becomes more strongly marked
between sacrifice and remembrance. The early Christian era
was very careful to stress the spirituality of their worship, just
as our Lord did when He said that the Father seeks those who
worship Him in 'spirit and in truth'. For this reason they
spoke almost exclusively of the *Eucharistia*. In the second
century *Eucharistia* was the name of the celebration and today
is the name of the sacrament which comes from it. In the
second century certain expressions appear among the apolo-
gists in which they explain: we Christians have no sacrifice at
all (i.e., not as the pagans have them). Minucius Felix wrote:
'We Christians have no altars and no temple' (that is, not as
you pagans have). 'The only homage that is pleasing to God,'
says Justin, 'is that we thank Him and send up on high through
the spirit hymns and songs of praise.' This was the reason why
in 1910 a bitter controversy arose between Franz Wieland and
Emil Dorsch to the effect that before Irenaeus (i.e., before the
end of the second century) no other sacrifice at all was known
in the Church except that which was contained in the thanksgiving-prayer. It was not difficult to show that a thanksgiving
prayer over bread and wine was in fact meant, and that with it
a gift was offered to God and that therefore a sacrifice was
certainly intended.

A little later we find the idea of sacrifice prominent in the

writings of Irenaeus, and even strongly emphasized. We find
the word *offerre* even in the oldest Mass formula of Hippolytus
In the first half of the Eucharistic prayer the dominant ideas
are Thanksgiving and Memorial. But after the words of consecration we find: *Memores igitur mortis et resurrectionis eius
offerimus tibi panem et calicem.* So is the act of sacrifice expressed.
This is expressed in the same way in the present Canon, only a
little less formally, *offerimus praeclarae maiestati tuae . . . panem
sanctum vitae aeternae et calicem salutis perpetuae.* There is no
reason to suppose that this line of thought was not customary
in the Eucharistic Prayer long before Hippolytus. But this
much is correct: towards the end of the second century the
emphasis shifted. Up to that time the main emphasis was on
the prayer of thanksgiving, but now it shifts to the sacrifice.
It appears that this was connected with the fact that, mean-
time, inside the Church a sect had become widely dangerous;
a sect which went in for emphasizing the spirituality of
Christian worship as far as it could, namely Gnosticism. The
gnostic was a kind of enlightened Christian; the spirit was the
only thing that was of any value. Everything material was
worthless and from the devil. The visible creation could not
have come from God at all. Now the Doctors of the Church
begin to defend matter and the visible creation. Irenaeus is
their most important champion. They begin to stress that
even the Christian worship, however spiritual it may be, has
its beginnings in matter. Christ Himself chose 'the bread
which comes from creation' and the 'chalice which comes
from our creation', and so taught His disciples the new
offering. Now there develops in the rite a strong emphasis
both by words and by the external action on material gifts.
Even before the words of consecration, the visible gift is
named and offered to God as a visible expression of our
thanksgiving; *Te igitur . . . rogamus et petimus uti accepta
habeas.* Indeed even the bringing up of the gift and the placing
of it on the altar, which up to then had been done before the
Thanksgiving-prayer without any formality, assumed the
form of a liturgical act, the offertory. The gifts are solemnly
brought up in some way or other, and the faithful are allowed
to bring up the bread and wine. In the third century the

offertory procession appears, and when the gifts are placed on the altar, a special prayer is said over them before the thanks-giving-prayer, the *oratio super oblata*, the Secret prayer. In this way the offertory was built up into a full liturgical act.

This led to a gradual change; the title *Eucharistia* began to disappear. It was used more and more only for the sacrament, which comes from the celebration. The sacred action itself since the fourth century was called by preference *oblatio* or *sacrificium* (in Greek προσφορα). The change even affected the interior arrangements of the church building. Up to then the altar had never been fixed in one place. Only a table was necessary and this was brought out as required and set up for Mass. The altar has never had in Christian worship that religious meaning which it possessed in pagan times and among the Jews; in those times a gift was made holy only when it had come into contact with the altar. In Christendom the final gift, the Body and Blood of Christ, is already sacred in itself and needs no holiness from the altar. The altar is really only a technical device on which the gifts may be made. It is only as a matter of secondary importance given a special consecration. The *cathedra* of the Bishop, who as a rule was the celebrant, seemed to be much more important than the altar. The bishop, who spoke the *Eucharistia* over the gifts of bread and wine which were laid before him, is the real focus; the bishop as the liturgist and also the teacher and shepherd of his flock. Now one began to emphasise the material gifts, and even the material supports assumed an importance. Where there was once a table, casually erected and afterwards taken away, there is now a massive structure belonging to the essentials of the church, a Christian altar rich in history, no longer made out of wood (although wooden altars are still found well into the Middle Ages), but out of hard stone. It was at once a symbol of Christ (*petra autem erat Christus*), but covered to such an extent by the baldachino and built upon in the form of gradines and a triptych that the original idea of the altar has almost disappeared.

The consequences of this had its effect on the liturgical shaping of the Ordo of the Mass. I have mentioned the offertory, but inside the Canon there is also a change to be mentioned: the insertion of petitions into the Canon. Petitions have always been connected with the Eucharistic celebration. We have Justin's word for it that on Sundays, after the Scripture readings and the sermon, everyone stood up and prayed for all the cares and concerns of the Church. Only then were the gifts brought forward. Now, since the middle of the fourth century, these petitions were daringly inserted into the Great Prayer itself, the *Canon Actionis*. This was done in various ways: before the consecration and before the *Sanctus*, as in Egypt; after the consecration as in Syria and Byzantium; before the consecration and (in certain circumstances) even after the consecration, as in the Roman liturgy.

This may likewise be connected with the stronger emphasis on sacrifice. When one has in mind particularly the thanksgiving-prayer, and when all one's attention is directed towards thanking and praising God for His benefits and especially for His work of salvation through Christ, one does not immediately think of joining petitions to it. The case is otherwise when we have eyes only for the sacrificial gift, and a precious gift at that. Then one's thoughts turn more easily to the idea of a return for which one could pray. Petitions were added on in this way: *Te igitur rogamus ac petimus—uti accepta habeas haec dona*, and one immediately continues, *inprimis quae tibi offerimus*. . . . Here a handle is given for all the names and groups which one wishes to include and for all the causes which one wishes to recommend. A framework is thus fashioned in the Roman Canon for both names and petitions, and the forms which we have today are essentially those which were fixed in the fourth and fifth centuries. Within the Universal Church the Pope and the Bishop are named, and as a consequence all the names of the shepherds who guard the true, Catholic and apostolic Faith, and all those *qui offerunt hoc sacrificium laudis*, are also mentioned; that is, all present who are at the same time offerers. Then certain special offerers are mentioned by name; but the Church does not stop short at these names of casual and personal offerers. Right from the beginning the whole Church is included, and so the circle is widened; the officers who are present offer *communicantes* in communion even with the whole Church

Triumphant. There follows in the text, which was fixed in the sixth century, a symbolical series of saints: twelve apostles and twelve particularly famous martyrs, and at their head Mary, the Mother of God.

In the same way after the consecration a space is left for the names of the dead. In former times this was not done at every Mass, and certainly not at the Sunday Mass. The names are no longer of those *qui offerunt*. The dead cannot offer any more, so the text reads: 'Remember them also' (*Memento etiam*), 'Give them also a share.' They can no more themselves receive *ex hac participatione* the Body and Blood of Our Lord as we may, but give them also a share, and finally us *nobis quoque peccatoribus*. This refers to those who say this prayer at the altar, and here as well, just as at the *Communicantes*, union with the Church Triumphant is sought. Once again a symbolical series of saints is cited: seven men and seven women martyrs, and at their head John the Baptist, the second leader in the company of saints whom Our Lord Himself called the greatest of those who had been born of woman.

In the Canon there is another place for names, not only names but also petitions, and as a framework for these we have the *Hanc igitur*. Perhaps sometimes an embarrassing situation arose here when the faithful recommended petitions, the mention of which would not have suited the sacred text. At present a formula remains which includes only quite universal petitions, and this has been the case since Gregory the Great: *diesque nostros in tua pace disponas atque ab aeterna damnatione nos eripi, et in electorum tuorum iubeas grege numerari.*

We must say a few words about the final liturgical development, which was a result of the emphasis on the sacrificial character of the Mass, and which in the course of the Middle Ages was considerably amplified—the Offertory. The liturgical movement of recent decades has not been very favourably disposed towards the offertory, chiefly because it is so easily misinterpreted on account of the name 'offertory', as though the sacrifice is already completed, which of course it is not until the consecration. In devising forms for Community Mass these considerations have had their importance. One should speak rather of a making ready, of a preparation of the gifts. Sometimes this antipathy has gone so far that the offertory procession has been disapproved of. Nevertheless, I am of the opinion that we ought to see the positive value, the real meaning of the action of the offertory.

The sacrifice of Christ is not of course enacted here; but in every sense the offertory does prepare the way for it. He Himself has so arranged it that we should take the things of this earth in order to offer His sacrifice. We, the Church, should go before Him with our earthly gifts from which He deigns to prepare His gifts. The Christian sacrifice begins essentially with bread and wine. Therein lies a twofold symbolism (and this on the authority of Divine Institution). The sacrifice which we offer, however sacred and heavenly it is, does not sway above our heads in the clouds, but the material world is made use of, material creation is reverenced in it, and it is made holy and brought back to God. Secondly, our human life in particular is taken up in these gifts; the work of our hands, the food from which we live and therefore our life itself. Our earthly life on this earth, with all its wants and necessities, is caught up in these earthly gifts; but in gifts the value of which has been raised up to the value of heavenly gifts with which nothing can be compared. They demand from us thanksgiving, adoration and the most interior offering of the heart.

The offertory therefore is a thoroughly valuable integrating part of the structure of the Mass-liturgy, and its introduction in the third century must be considered a step forward in the development of the liturgy. Coming down to particulars we must distinguish two acts in the offertory: the bringing up of the gifts, and the placing and blessing of the gifts on the altar.

The existence of this action of bringing up the gifts is known from roughly the third to the fourth century in all liturgies, but in the Roman it developed into a procession. The offertory chant in our missals is a relic, which can only be explained by its use as a chant to accompany the procession Certainly this offertory procession cannot be reintroduced in parish churches as a daily or even as a Sunday event. But it would have some importance, if at least the bringing up of the gifts could be given some kind of form, especially on Sundays. Not only the cruets with the wine and water, but also the hosts (at least those for the communion of the faithful) ought in some way to be carried up to the altar in a formal and solemn way.

The second act of the offertory is the placing of the gifts on the altar, accompanied by various prayers. The oldest prayer which even today is the most important, the *Oratio super Oblata* or the Secret Prayer, has already been mentioned. But since the ninth century many other prayers have been added, and up to the end of the Middle Ages many more prayers than we have today, especially in our countries. In Italy they were rather more cautious. There they took over the offertory prayers which had been introduced in the north up to the eleventh century; these are our present offertory prayers: a prayer over the bread, a prayer over the chalice. Then the general offering, which hints at the meaning of the offertory, is spoken with emphasis and in an inclined position, *In spiritu humilitatis*. There follows then a petition that according to circumstances, our offering may meet with blessing from above: *Veni sanctificator*. Then a second general offering, spoken in the same sense and in a similar inclined position: *Suscipe Sancta Trinitas*. One ought not to attribute too much importance to these prayers alone. They are never spoken out loud; they are only words of accompaniment, and possess much the same value as the prayers which are said when the priest vests.

This is also clear because the exhortation to prayer addressed to the faithful in the *Orate Fratres* is spoken afterwards, just before the proper and ancient oratio, the *Oratio super Oblata*. At a Community Mass, therefore, if any prayer is to be said out loud at the offertory, it should in the *Suscipiat* rather than the other prayers which precede it.

Nevertheless these preceding prayers share in the function of the *Oratio super Oblata*. The whole of the offertory signifies an introductory offering, a kind of pre-dedication, which is given to the gifts even before the consecration, just as the chalice, the paten, the altar and the house of God itself is dedicated beforehand, before it is used for holy purposes.

From this the sacrifice of the Church originates. Of course it would mean little or nothing if it were not the beginning of the sacrifice which the Church in praise and thanksgiving offers together with Christ: *offerimus memores passionis eius.*

CHAPTER III

PLEBS SANCTA

WE have studied in detail the two characteristic features of
the Christian worship and of the Mass in particular. The Mass
is a service of remembrance and thanksgiving; it is also an
ascent to God in sacrifice. We must now consider more
closely a third dimension, and we find its classical expression in
the same place where we found the first two characteristics:
nos servi tui sed et plebs tua sancta. Of course the *servi tui* cannot
perform the sacred worship themselves; a *plebs sancta* in some
form or other is essential, which gives to the Mass liturgy and
to Christian liturgy in general a stamp of its own.

In ancient pagan religious worship it was not essential,
although there were exceptions, for the people to take part in
the act of worship. For this there existed a priesthood which
looked after everything. Even the place of worship was laid
out in accordance with this idea. It was not a room in which
people could gather, but an ancient temple housing in its
interior quite a small sanctuary, a gloomy cell, where the
picture of the gods was placed. The rest of the building was
concerned simply with external decoration, rows of columns,
the whole thing a facade to cover up the sanctuary. Even in
Jerusalem the temple was only slightly different, but at least
there were vestibules, spare places in front of the sanctuary
which were meant for the people. In Christianity the place
appointed for worship was originally, and still is, essentially a
place for the assembled people, for the *Ecclesia*, which is a
sancta Ecclesia, a priestly people which has itself been called to
come before God, which through Christ has access to God.
Therefore the Christian place of worship is essentially an
interior building, appointed to house the Christian community. Its beauty develops within itself, and it is always a
suspicious sign when the Christian place of worship begins to
develop externally as a building (e.g., the Gothic).

This basic principle of Christian worship has become in many ways decisive for the shape of the liturgy, for its externals as well as for what concerns its inner sphere. The words *Plebs sancta* belong to this inner sphere; for if we describe the Mass as essentially remembrance and sacrifice, a subject for both these actions presents itself in the words: *nos servi tui sed et plebs tua sancta*. Both *memores* and *offerimus* are related to this double subject, Thy servants and Thy holy people. Even the *offerre*, the most sacred act in the whole of christian worship, is the work of the people gathered together. As you know, this point is gone into in some detail in the encyclical *Mediator Dei*. There an exact interpretation of this point is given. Of course the people cannot consecrate, but it does not follow that the people cannot offer. In ancient times the people were denied without any justification the offering as well as the consecrating, because these two ideas were not sufficiently clearly distinguished.

But let us enquire a little more closely how this principle of Christian worship, according to which the people is the subject, develops in the wider province of the liturgy, especially the Mass liturgy. First of all we must acknowledge the fact that all the prayers which constitute the proper official Mass liturgy are in the plural without exception. There are, it is true, in the present *Ordo* of the Mass certain prayers which are in the singular; quite a number of them in fact, even if we exclude words taken from the psalms: *Introibo, Lavabo*. But all these prayers do not belong to the ancient structure of the Mass liturgy. They are never spoken in a loud voice. They have never been anything but private prayers of the celebrant, most of them prayers accompanying actions. They were first introduced in the Carolingian period on Frankish soil, where there was the conception of the Gallic liturgy: there must be no pauses in the liturgy. The priest when he is doing anything, when he approaches the altar, when he lays gifts upon the altar, when he prepares himself for Holy Communion, when he leaves the altar, must always be saying a prayer. But these prayer texts were not constituent parts of public worship; they practically never appeared in a missal. They were passed on by word of mouth, and for this reason whenever they were written down, were written down with many variations in the text. They were intended rather as aids to the personal devotion of the priest, and as such we may value them.

Nevertheless, they are easily distinguishable, even externally, from the prayers which belong to the real structure of the Mass liturgy. They are not said like these in an attitude of prayer, but either purely incidentally during some kind of external action, or else with hands joined—the attitude of prayer of the younger German peoples. In northern lands these prayers were at once incorporated in the Roman liturgy as soon as the Roman liturgy was taken over in the eighth century. When later this Roman-Frankish liturgy flowed back from the north towards Rome in the tenth and eleventh centuries (chiefly through the expeditions to Rome of the German Emperor, but also through the Cluny movement), these prayers were also accepted in Rome and later were prescribed for the whole of Christendom.

There is no need for us to despise or underestimate these prayers. But if we wish to see the structure of the Roman liturgy in its true light, we must consider these prayers as a secondary element, as so much decoration and make-weight, which has been put in by way of supplement. The ancient, basic Roman structure of the Mass includes, therefore, only the prayers from *Sursum Corda* down to the *Pax Domini*; in the essential preface, therefore, and Canon, with the *Pater noster* at the end. We must add to that the three variable prayers: collect, secret and post-communion. These prayers the priest says alone. The old sacramentaries (the priest's mass-book) contain nothing but the Canon and the texts of the three prayers for every Sunday and feast day (and also the various texts for the Preface). All these texts are in the plural.

We may observe, however, that to say these prayers in the name of all, and thus in the plural, was not considered sufficient. One also made sure of the express assent and joint action of the congregation. Here we have a very ancient Christian tradition which can be traced back without hesitation to the apostles and also, partly, to the customs of the synagogue. The assent of the people was required

in the Amen. Even at the beginning of the prayer, measures
were taken to see that the people were included and that
they knew that they were included. Before the priest begins
the prayer he invites everyone's attention: *Oremus, Gratias
agamus*. Even before the *Oremus, Gratias agamus*, the people
are not addressed simply by *Fratres, oremus*, but by a religious greeting, which the people answer in return. Before the thanksgiving prayer the summons is still more
imperative; but it is no mere greeting but an exhortation:
Sursum corda.

This is the case, or almost so, in all liturgies—sometimes
even more forcibly expressed. We are dealing here with a
tradition from the early period of the Church, an essential
characteristic of all Christian liturgies. Various acclamations
then are required of the people, through which it expresses
its participation and assent to the prayers of the liturgy which
are said in its name.

Bound up with this is another factor: the chants of the
Ordinary. At once we must state that the word 'chants' is to
be taken in a very broad sense; in the same sense as we speak
of the chanting by the priest. The priest has to say the prayers
out loud; because they are more or less invariable, formal
texts, the loud declamation of them becomes almost a chant.
Ancient rhetoricians trained the speaker to allow his speech in
certain places, especially near the end, to be chanted. As in the
case of the priest singing at the altar, it was a question originally
of a mere reciting note varied with a few cadences. This is
particularly obvious in the case of the oldest chant of the
Ordinary which the people shared, the *Sanctus*; especially
when it is sung to one of the oldest melodies, the SANCTUS
of plainsong mass XVIII, also used in a Requiem Mass. It is
my opinion that if we are to give back to the people a chant
(and if more than a hymn at the beginning and end of the
Mass can be attempted) then it ought to be the *Sanctus*, in Latin
or English. Here the text itself urges the whole congregation
to join in: *Cum quibus et nostras voces*. Moreover, in the ancient
liturgy and even in the Carolingian period it was the custom
not only for the people, but the priest with the people, to
sing, or more correctly for the people to join in, the altar-

chant of the priest; because the *Sanctus* is also the priest's chant. For this reason it is still to be found in all the ancient sacramentaries, while the *Kyrie* and *Agnus Dei* are wanting.

The *Sanctus* therefore is the oldest and most important chant of the Ordinary. The rest of the texts of the Ordinary belonging to the people are to be found within the Fore-Mass, with the exception of a single text which belongs to later elements, the *Agnus Dei*, introduced about the year 700 as a chant to accompany the breaking of the bread. But quite apart from the reason for its introduction into the Mass, the *Agnus Dei* can also be conceived as a greeting of the Sacrament at the end of the Canon. When the Canon has been concluded and the offering done with (the *Pater noster* is reckoned inclusively in this case), it is the proper time to greet the Body of the Lord in the Sacrament; similarly on Maundy Thursday after the consecration of the Holy Oils, there is the greeting, *Ave Sanctum Chrisma*. With the cry of *Agnus Dei*, the sacrificed Body of the Lord is signified in the Sacred Host, which is later shown to the people at the *Ecce Agnus Dei*.

In the Fore-Mass the texts of the Ordinary which belong to the people are more strongly represented. This is to some extent understandable, for here at the beginning of the Mass the community must, as it were, take shape. The totality which has now become present has to manifest itself; it has to pray itself and sing itself into a unity. Only then does the person whose vocation it is to pray and offer sacrifice come foward and lead the assembly. So it has been from the earliest times (since roughly the fifth century) that the first thing that could be heard at the beginning of Mass was the *Kyrie* litany, where the invocations were spoken by the clergy or by one cleric, and the people answered with the *Kyrie eleison*. Then as always happens when something has to be cut, all that remained was the *Kyrie eleison* and the *Christe eleison*. Here it is to be noticed that both invocations are addressed to Christ; He is the '*Kyrios*', and it is He whom we call upon at the beginning of the celebration dedicated to His memory. The notion that this threefold *Kyrie* is a reference to the Trinity, is only late Carolingian; I think that it ought to be abandoned. It produces complications and has too little foundation in fact. It was understandable at the time as an after-effect of the controversies which were directed towards the heresies against the Trinity. Such a liturgical polemic has long since been unnecessary. This interpretation only obscures the context. The *Kyrie* here is only introduced as what we may describe as an up-beat before the Oratio, just as on many occasions today it acts as an up-beat before the best of all prayers, the Lord's prayer, the *Pater noster*; *Kyrie eleison*, *Christie eleison*, *Kyrie eleison*, *Pater noster*. First the call to prayer of the whole people, a call to Christ, then the Orations which the priest directs towards God *per Christum*.

On occasions when a more festive mood is to be stressed, on all Sundays and feastdays, there is added immediately after the *Kyrie*, which possesses a serious character and is after all a cry for mercy, a proper chant, a simple but powerful people's chant, a hymn, the *Gloria in excelsis*. It was already widespread in the fourth century. In Rome it was used but sparingly, although among the Franks it was very common, and this more common usage became finally the standard. It is a real people's chant. The oldest melodies are very simple, and any-one could easily master them. The *Gloria*, then, is a hymn which only adds festive colouring to that up-beat before the Oratio, a people's prayer and a people's chant, the aspirations of which are all summed up in the Oratio.

But within the Fore-mass we find two further instances of singing. These are genuine songs,—in fact, artistic music— wherein, however, the people were originally intended to have some part. I refer to the chants between the readings and the Introit. They are not Ordinary chants intended originally for the people, but Proper chants belonging to a well-trained choir of singers, or even to one singer.

Of all the Proper chants the oldest are those which come between the readings from Scripture. We find them in all liturgies in one form or another. They are a relic of the time when there were at least three readings in every Mass (the Gradual came after the first, the Alleluia verse after the second), and also a relic from the time when there was no specially trained choir even in the cathedrals. Up to at least the fourth century real artistic chant with a choir and instruments was rejected as pagan and worldly. But there was one singer, one cantor, whose function it was to sing the psalm. The people were to combine with this cantor by singing an invariable verse, once at the beginning and then after every verse of the psalm. We still have this method in its original form in the Invitatory psalm of the breviary. The structure of responsorial chant, as it is called, is also clearly seen in the alleluia verse; and even here the response of the people (where the people have been liturgically educated) could easily be introduced. The alleluia could be said or sung by the Cantor and then taken up by the people; after the verse it should be repeated by the people once again.

The second place in the Proper chants where the people still participated until quite recently was the *Gloria Patri* at the Introit. The rubrics of the Carolingian period require, amongst other things, the people to sing (apart from the *Sanctus*) this *Gloria Patri*. Indeed in one place found amongst the more ancient rubrics of the Dominican liturgy, the *Gloria Patri* at the Introit was reckoned as part of the chants of the Ordinary even in the thirteenth century, as well as the usual *Kyrie, Gloria, Credo, Sanctus* and *Agnus Dei*. It was not desirable to have so long a chant as the Introit without the people having at least some sort of opportunity for participation, and so the *Gloria Patri* was assigned to the people and later to the monastic choir. It seems indeed, that originally this *Gloria Patri* was added to the psalms to give an opportunity of participation to those who did not know the psalms by heart. This was so in the fourth century, chiefly in the East in Antioch.

The communal character of the Mass-liturgy is seen at its strongest, as might be expected, in the section called simply 'Communion'. Here we see the *Plebs Sancta*, as such, really assume an importance, since it is called to a sacred meal.

The older ones among us have grown up accustomed to the attitude that Holy Communion is a purely personal matter, that it concerns only the person who has just received the Lord's Body; and with this idea in mind the word *communio* was understood and explained in such a way that it meant merely the union of the individual with Christ, as though it were a *Co-unio*. A great deal has been written about the idea of communion; but at any rate this much is certain: Communion—κοινωνια—does not refer to any kind of union, a meeting of two people, but a community, an alliance, the togetherness of many. The Church is such a community. The Church does not have communion with the saints for she is herself a communion of saints. She is the *Communio Sanctorum*, and the *sacra communio* of the Eucharist is only a visible expression of it. All those who are in the fullest sense members of the Church through the life of grace are invited to share this sacred meal which follows the sacrifice. The idea is thoroughly scriptural and Pauline: 'For we, being many, are one bread and one body: all that partake of one bread.' (1 Cor. 10 17.)

The social character of the Church and especially of the Church's worship is, after a long period of individualism, slowly forcing its way more clearly into the consciousness of the present generation. And as is always the case with new discoveries, the resultant enthusiasm easily leads to exaggerations. At least one must be careful not to be drawn into opposite extremes. In many places the idea has emerged that the meal, the social meal must be considered as the one and only basic form of the Mass; it is not the sacrifice, but the meal which determines the basic form of the Holy Mass. There is a table; bread and wine are put on it, one eats and one drinks. What are we to say to this? That the meal is an equally determining factor in the shaping of the whole Mass, and not just in the communion part of the Mass, is quite clear. It may also be conceded that if we are to trust the evidence of our eyes, then the basic form does in fact appear to be the meal, and almost entirely the meal (almost, because there were certain oblation rites existing right from the beginning, rites which express the sacrifice of the Church).But if we look at the whole of the Mass-liturgy, where the Word, the word of thanksgiving, of praise, of consecration is decisive, which through the Word becomes an *Oblatio rationabilis*, then one cannot overlook the fact that the Mass is essentially and, I would say, predominantly an offering, planned as a sacrifice, which overflows in the form of a meal. The meal is previously consecrated and carried to God. This movement to God, the *Eucharistia*, determines the entire character of the celebration.

The body of the Mass-celebration consists of the Preface and the Canon, in other words of the Eucharistic Prayer which in all liturgies is introduced with the summons: *Gratias agamus Domino Deo nostro*. It does not say: *Epulemur in Domino*, but *Gratias agamus*. Of course the thesis can be defended that the meal is the basic form in this way (as Joseph Pascher does), that the Eucharistic Prayer is explained as the grace before meals, and the fore-Mass as expressing the family spirit at table. But this is only a quarrel about words. If I say that the consecrated meal which is dedicated and offered up to God is the basic form, as far as facts are concerned it is the same as saying that it is an offering which concludes with a meal.

Bound up with this meal-aspect of the Mass is the question of what attitude one should take towards the *altare versus populum*—the altar facing the people. I do not intend to take sides rigidly one way or the other; but perhaps this is the place to have a look at the various views concerning it. As far as the rubrics and Canon law are concerned, the position of the altar *versus populum* is entirely justified, at least provided the Bishop raises no objection. Even apart from these considerations it is reasonable to say that the *altare versus populum* is indicated when a strong, clear spirit of unity exists among those present; when a general Communion of all is such an understood thing that the communal sacred meal is a genuine expression of their oneness. For example in a youth group or in a gathering like ours; it could also become the custom where because of the poverty and reduced circumstances, there is a more familiar atmosphere, as is often the case in the Diaspora.

But in the average parish at daily Mass where no special emphasis is laid on the meal, we must bear in mind that the Mass is not solely a communion-service. If the Mass were only a communion-service or only a service of the Word, as in Protestant churches, then it would always have to be done *versus populum*; for the word too is spoken to the people, just

[1] In the St. Rita Church in Berlin, Mass was celebrated *versus populum* during the Study Week.

as communion is given to the people. But the Mass is essentially a sacrifice, a coming into the presence of God, during which the priest stands at the head of the procession. The assembled congregation is not yet so much of an enclosed community that it can repose completely in itself. It has found Christ in God, but it has not yet found Him in His fullness. The Church is still a pilgrim, she is still on the way to God, afflicted by much distress. Thus it might be more correct midst average conditions to hold on to the traditional position as the general norm, and to consider the other solution as an exception; an exception which one can only hope will be made use of as often as possible.

There is of course also the pedagogical point of view when for reasons of religious instruction a class of school-children gathers round the altar. Of course the great distance of the altar from the mass of the people will have to be overcome, at least in the sense that the altar must become once more the focal point to which the whole of the congregation is directed.

The position of the altar is naturally connected with the question: what is after all the ideal form of the church? Should it be a round building or a processional church? At any rate it is surprising that a round building has never really taken root in the history of church architecture; one can only point to exceptions which, especially during the Baroque period, were more common. When a round building was chosen for a church what usually happened was that the altar did not take up a central position, but was set up in a special niche in the periphery of the building, especially in the East.

It must be observed that the basic structure of the Church and of her religious worship reveals itself in these details. The Church is a community, a community of saints; but she is also a graded community whose members consist of the clergy and the people. And so we have the building of the church divided up into the space for the clergy, who by the authority of their divine mission possess leadership and power, called the sanctuary, and the space for the people called the nave. This corresponds exactly to the words of the Canon; it is not simply the *Plebs sancta* who is mentioned as the subject of the celebration but: *nos servi tui, sed et plebs tua sancta*.

We must now enquire into the style and manner of the communion part of the Mass and see how it was liturgically conceived. It deals with the communion itself as well as its more remote preparation. The *Pater noster* is chiefly intended as preparation for holy communion, first of all because of the petition for daily bread, and also because of the petition for forgiveness. This petition for forgiveness and freeing from all evils is continued in the Embolism (*Libera nos quaesumus*) and the prayer is concluded with the *Per Dominum nostrum*. We take the 'Our Father' out of the mouth of Our Lord and through Him offer it to Our Father in Heaven, as we do with other prayers.

A secondary preparatory act is the Kiss of Peace. The cry *Pax Domini* was the signal for all the faithful to greet one another with the kiss. The *Et cum Spiritu tuo* carries with it the assent to this Kiss of Peace. In our present Mass-liturgy the Pax-prayer and the giving of the Kiss of Peace have unfortunately become divorced from each other and are now separated by the *Agnus Dei*.

In the East the people are now invited to receive Holy Communion with the cry: 'The Holy to the holy.' An analogy was introduced into our Roman liturgy in the sixteenth century in the *Ecce Agnus Dei* just before Communion.

From these preparatory acts for communion we distinguish the rite which enshrines communion itself. It will perhaps be more intelligible if we consider it parallel with the rite of the offertory. In the offertory we have the bringing up of the gifts in the form of a procession; in the communion we have the reception of the gifts also in a procession. During the offertory procession the Offertory text is chanted, just as during the communion the Communion verse is chanted. In each case the action is concluded by an Oratio from the priest; in the first case the Secret prayer, in the other the Post-Communion. Both prayers are composed in the same style and method, and are said in the same way. Previously in both cases the priest has prayed in a low voice in words and phrases which come from the Carolingian era.

And so the whole celebration is brought to its conclusion by the sacred meal; the *plebs sancta* has been drawn together by new bonds and sanctified anew by the Bread of Heaven.

When we utter the words *Plebs sancta* and follow their meaning as we have done through the Mass-liturgy, must we not admit a few misgivings? We have been sketching an ideal picture of the holy people of God gathered together round God to worship Him 'in spirit and in truth' and to share in this sacred meal, but in reality the congregation considered as a whole is not at all so holy. There are sinners among them, men who are living in sin, and perhaps they are not individual exceptions, and yet we expect and demand the whole parish to appear at Mass on Sundays. And then some realists give tongue, and seek to recall us from litrugical romanticism to sober reality. Prof. Johannes Auer of Bonn writes an exhaustive essay on Spiritual Communion, and maintains that the right form of participation for the majority of our congregations is not actual communion but spiritual communion. A Frenchman, G. de Broglie, discusses the meaning of the words 'sacrificing Church' and holds that they do not refer to the congregation actually present but the whole Church, the Church which offers sacrifice through her priests. During a study-circle on this problem it was emphasized that the faithful very often have no understanding of the Holy Mass, because they no longer have any consciousness of guilt or of atonement, no feeling for sin. They must be taught to understand sin and the meaning of the sacrifice of atonement; but for this the idea of *Plebs sancta* is no use as a starting point or even basis.

What are we to say to all this? Is the Mass primarily and essentially a sacrificial offering of sinners? The wording of our Mass-liturgy protests against it. The Mass is not primarily the cult-celebration of sinners. The Mass is indeed a sacrifice of propitiation, as the Council of Trent emphasizes, but it is primarily the sacrifice of thanksgiving: *Gratias agamus*. It is the chant of praise of the redeemed, who were once sinners, but through Baptism (and if the occasion arises through Penance) have been cleansed from their sins, who have a right to join in the *Sanctus* with the angelic choirs and share in the Bread of Angels. The sacrifice on the Cross was primarily a sacrifice of atonement, offered for the redemption of the

world; the sacrifice on our altars is primarily a sacrifice of
thanksgiving by those who have been redeemed. We cannot
get away from these basic facts. We may not press the identity
of the sacrifice on the Cross and the sacrifice of the Mass so
far that these essential differences are obscured.

Yet we must keep the realities of life in mind. Those who
come from the world and enter the church have every reason
first to wipe away the dust from the feet. The ancient church
made allowances for this and had conscious transitional
stages: first the *atrium*, then the entrance hall and the door.

Even the liturgy allows for this fact. There is an act of
purification of some sort at the beginning; at least a symbolic
act of purification. Priests first of all wash their hands in the
sacristy and do it again at the beginning of the Mass of the
Faithful; they also say the *Confiteor* at the foot of the altar.
Even among the present plans and desires for reform in the
Ordo of the Mass this idea persists: there must be an act of
purification at the beginning. In the same place and for the
same reason the faithful take holy water at the entrance of the
church, and on Sundays the *Asperges* precedes Mass; the
Asperges is basically a renewal of Baptism: *Amplius lava me.*

In the Didache (*c.* 14, 1) the Sunday Mass was said to begin
with a confession of sins. It is a moot point whether this
means a sacramental confession by the whole congregation or
not. At any rate a thousand years later (eleventh century) after
the sermon on Sundays and feast days, before the beginning of
the Mass of the Faithful, the whole congregation was given a
general absolution and this *suppositis supponendis* as a sacramental absolution.

An act of purification belongs to the beginning of the
Mass, and we must not despise it but seek to give it a suitable
form. Besides, we must allow for the fact there are quite a
number of people present who have not been able to free
themselves from the snares of their sins; an act of purification
is not sufficient for them, but they do at least fulfill their
obligation of hearing Mass.

This case was provided for in the ancient Church in a
proper manner. In the Greek Eastern Church in the fourth
century there existed the συσταντεσ; that is those belonging

to the fourth and final penitential stage. Perhaps they were those who, because their sins were only private sins, were not condemned to stand amongst the penitents. They took their place among the faithful, but were not allowed to communicate. Such συσταντεσ we will always have with us. But we are still justified in vindicating for the liturgy the purity of its ideal, and in expressing this by saying: The Mass is the celebration of the *plebs sancta*.

Christians who are living with the life of grace should be joyously conscious of their Christian dignity and should receive new strength from this consciousness. But those who have not kept up to the standard ought also, from the celestial splendour and holy solemnity of the celebration, to be filled with contrition and holy regrets—for the Mass is the celebration of the *Plebs sancta*.

CHAPTER IV

SOCIA EXSULTATIONE

THIS title may appear at first sight rather curious. The words are well known to you. The Preface speaking of the Divine Majesty says: 'Heaven and the Powers of Heaven praise Thee with joy in chorus—*socia exsultatione concelebrant.*' But how are these words connected with our present theme? Well, the heavenly liturgy is the prototype of the earthly, and it is significant that even the earthly liturgy is celebrated with *socia exsultatio*; it is celebrated with great joy (*exsultatione*) by everyone (*socia*). But in practice these two ideals, here brought together, often stand in opposition to each other, like two poles having between them a tension of varying degree.

Our religious worship ought to be social worship, a communal celebration of all those who are gathered together. But the festive joy which is associated with social worship on special occasions (and in places where the liturgical life flourishes, thus giving to the liturgy itself a certain splendour) tends to become so highly developed that it becomes a threat to the social character of the liturgy. This is true of Church building; it is true of Church-music and Gregorian chant; it is true of speech and poetry in the liturgy, and it is true finally of liturgical ceremonial.

In general we may say that in the Roman liturgy a satisfactory compromise has been found between these two opposite points of view, although this may be realized in very different ways. In any case it will be useful to consider a few pertinent questions.

We are dealing here with the impulse, springing from the nature of man and the liturgy, to give to the liturgy a shape both beautiful and solemn. At the same time we must recognize the danger of excessive beauty and solemnity; in other words we must acknowledge the difficulties inseparable from a combination of culture and of what concerns the spiritual life. The spiritual life obviously is the more important, because it is the interior offering of oneself to God. But the interior must always find its expression in public worship. Only the best and the most beautiful are good enough for the public worship of God. It is only natural that with the tide of growing wealth and the growing taste for things cultural, liturgical rites will become ever richer. If I may put it this way, public worship which ought to be the expression of the minds and hearts of the faithful, is being put into an art gallery—an art gallery which tends to develop an independence and claim a value for itself alone. But this independence, this claiming of value for itself, will gradually stifle the inner spirit. What we are going to do now is examine the solemn liturgical forms for what they are, those forms which have developed in the liturgy in the course of centuries; we want to see them as they were before they lost their inner spirit and meaning, and we want to treat them even as we have inherited them in such a way that they will not lose their life and meaning. In short we are going to examine the beginnings of the liturgical rites and see what is essential in them.

The first wave of solemn liturgical forms in the grand style swept into the public worship of Christians with the Peace of the Church in 313. It was visible first of all in the construction of the church. The Church was offered wealth of all kinds, or rather the wealthy ruling-class, especially the Imperial Family themselves, began to establish magnificent buildings for the Church. We do not know what compromise was made between the high ideals of the founder and benefactor and the planning of the church, but at times a critical situation must certainly have arisen. The church had to remain a church, the holy church of Christ orientated towards the next life. On the other hand the wishes of the Imperial founder must have carried great weight, for it seems that it was precisely the idea of the Imperial Throne-room which dominated the planning of a basilica. Rows of pillars led to the *Cathedra*, which was literally a throne, and above it in place of the Emperor's portrait was a mosaic of Christ or a symbolic representation of Him in mosaic. Nevertheless a solution and form was found which was worthy of the church. The history of art shows that the ancient Christian basilica, when compared with churches of a later period, displays a great simplicity and severity. Little attention is paid to external decoration, and there is no tower, and only plain, smooth walls. The door invites entry, but even here there is first an ante-room which separates the basilica from the world. Only now is the beauty of the interior allowed to be seen, but it is a sober, clear beauty. It contains nothing that is flippant or purely ornamental. The forms of nature are missing, forms from the organic world, from the plant-world, which were used so richly later on in the Gothic and Baroque periods. Heinrich Lützeler says of the basilica: 'It exists without the world, it exists in spite of the world, it attracts men towards that which is interior.'

It is not my intention here to go into the history of church architecture in any detail. I only wish to mention a few points which concern the growing enrichment of all facets of public worship. The plan of a Roman church is direct and simple. It is ruled by strict laws, comparable to those of Gregorian chant; order and holy moderation are everywhere in evidence. The Gothic cathedral is itself much more highly developed; but even here one clear idea dominates. Hans Sedlmayr gives us an illuminating clue: 'there is a general or common desire to represent in the earthly church the *coelestis urbs Jerusalem* which, according to Apocalypse xxi, comes down from heaven.'

Hence we have the arrangement of the baldachino, of which the supports do not reach down to the earth. Hence the dissolution of the walls into the glowing colours of the stained-glass windows; hence a profusion of statues of the saints, who are all celestial beings. The Baroque cathedral from several aspects begins to assume a more secular outlook. The pictures of the saints in the paintings on the ceilings and on the altar become very naturalistic, not to say sensual.

The world of vital forms becomes broader. Everything sprouts and grows and flourishes, all with the very greatest splendour. The church becomes a festive hall, and even the word 'dance-hall' has been applied! But even through this rather secular mode of expression, there is one idea which persists through everything: the glorification of God and the triumph of the Church. Things become really bad in the nineteenth century when the age of imitations begins, when no longer does any clear idea dominate, when the forms of an earlier period once thrust aside are brought once more into use. The effect is doubled in a small church, where these reproductions accumulate in a small space and crowd one another out. At this point the idea of the *Ecclesia*, the *Plebs Sancta* which ought to be worshipping publicly, is seriously imperilled by these products of a past culture. The parish priest in such circumstances finds himself confronted with the difficult task of trying to create a clear pattern out of chaos, and yet he has to avoid acquiring the reputation of an iconoclast.

A special case important in this connection is the construction of the altar. The impulse to decorate the altar in every possible way goes back to the days of Christian antiquity. In fact we find Chrysostom saying that Christ ought rather to be clothed in the person of the poor than be overdressed on the altar with cloths inlaid with precious stones. (The table of the altar used to be covered with precious cloths from which were later derived the large expensive antependia.)

Now obviously the greatest reverence is due to the altar, even to the Christian altar, although it is not so essential as the altar in pre-Christian worship. The question is whether the real idea of the altar is visible, especially when we consider the development of the superstructure of the altar with its reredos, triptychs, gradines, etc. The superstructure of the altar, whatever shape it may take, is of secondary importance. As a result of the devotion paid to relics in the Middle Ages, relics and also reliquaries were placed on the altar; the relics of the saints are indeed worthy of a place on the *mensa*. But then pictures of saints to whom the church or the altar were dedicated were also placed on the *mensa Domini*. These reliquaries and portraits were gradually united more closely with the actual *mensa*, and so there arose the triptychs as well as the huge Baroque altars; for the art-historian perhaps often wonderful instances of Christian art, but for the liturgist and for the pastor of souls, an eclipse, almost a negation, of the true idea of the altar, especially when the altar appears as a mere appendage in this enormous structure. From a religious point of view surely it is better that a priest should celebrate Mass on a bare wooden table without any decoration or embellishment whatever.

It is unfortunate, I think, when the theme of the super-structure of the altar is the glorification of the saints. In most cases we cannot reverse these developments. But when Christian antiquity began to embellish the rear wall of the altar, more exactly the wall behind the altar (the *apsis*), it was at least expressing the Christ-Mystery. There was some picture or symbol of Christ, such as the jewelled Cross; and only subordinate to this was there any representation of redeemed mankind, such as the deer drinking from the heavenly fountains.

In conclusion, we may say that the ideal for a figurate decoration for the rear wall behind the altar would run as follows. What the Eucharistic Prayer, the great Prayer of Thanksgiving, praises in words ought to be expressed in pictorial form; what is already mentioned or hinted at in the *Anamnesis*, the memorial of the Passion, the resurrection and ascension, in short the theme of Easter, which is at the same time the eschatological theme and the theme of every Sunday. It should give us an insight into our glorified saviour and His Kingdom, Who through His death has passed into glory and has begun to gather His people about Him.

The growth in solemnity of Christian worship after the Church Peace of 313 revealed itself quite naturally in the ritual of the Church. We may mention here the chant sung during the entrance of the clergy, the Introit, at the beginning of Mass (this took place in the Roman as well as in other liturgies). Earlier, even during the time of Augustine, the Mass began quite simply with Scripture readings, as still happens at the beginning of the Good Friday liturgy. In order to understand the introduction of the Introit, we must imagine the vast buildings of Constantine; we must realise too that the clergy of various ranks and the papal court had become more numerous. Thus it is easy to understand the

entrance of the clergy into the church becoming an independent and meaningful act. The procession moved through the
main aisle and was treated as part of the liturgical rite. It was
given the same shape as the offertory procession and communion procession. The procession was accompanied by a
song, here the Introit; it closed with a prayer, the Collect.
Then something else was added immediately before the
Collect; the people prayed or sang the *Kyrie* litany and when
prescribed, the *Gloria*; finally came the Collect. The most
significant innovation here was the Entrance Song, the
Introit, and for the first time in the history of the Christian
liturgy the SCHOLA CANTORUM (choir of singers) is mentioned,
singing this Introit and later the offertory chant and the communion verse. As the clergy wended their way towards the
altar the *Schola Cantorum* sang a psalm suitable to the feast-
day, not responsorially as had been the custom, but anti-
phonally. Antiphonal chant consists simply of two choirs
or half-choirs standing opposite ($'\alpha\nu\tau\iota$) one another and
singing ($\varphi\omega\nu\eta$). The psalm is then divided up in such a way
that the verses are sung by each half-choir in turn as is done
even to-day when the office is sung in choir. To afford a
more suitable introduction to the psalm, the so-called antiphons were developed.

We must remember that musical instruments were for-
bidden; they were too much involved with the pagan style of
worship, and thus only the human voice came under consideration. The mood was set for the ensuing chant in the
following way: the text was intoned by a cantor, who gave
the note in a musical as well as in a spiritual sense. These words
of intonation had much to do with plainsong becoming an
art. This was true of ordinary psalm-singing, but particularly
of the solemn psalmody of the Mass. Early on, the Introit
developed a rich style; the psalm followed, to which was
added the *Gloria Patri* set to a simple tune (the *Gloria Patri*
was for some time sung by the people as we have seen); the
antiphon was then repeated. In the papal Stational churches, of
the seventh to eighth century, the psalm was sung until the
Pope gave the signal for it to stop. It soon became the general
custom to shorten the psalm, until finally only one verse

and the *Gloria Patri* remained, the antiphon of course being sung at the beginning and at the end. But even today when the Introit is sung as it should be, this one verse of the psalm is divided between a cantor or cantors and the choir, just as if there were still two verses. This abbreviation was carried to its furthest extent with the offertory and communion verses; only the antiphon is left. Previously a psalm was sung after both antiphons, usually the same as had been sung at the Introit. This is occasionally done to-day.

The introduction of antiphonal singing and the employment of the *Schola Cantorum* in these three places we can well understand. These were three places where an external action took up time, where there was a pause in prayer. But the eagerness of the singers did not remain satisfied with this. The Schola soon arrogated to itself the responsorial singing between the readings. This was done by retaining the Cantor (who was now a member of the Schola) but by taking over the Schola the responsories which used to belong to the people. It is well known that the most ornate passages in the whole of Gregorian chant are to be found in the Gradual, response and *Alleluia* verse. It is significant that the book in which these chants are contained has taken its name from the melismatic chants found between the Scripture readings, the *Graduale Romanum*. Earlier on these chants were contained in a proper book, in the Cantor's book, the *Cantorium*. The book for the rest of the Proper chants was called the Antiphonal or *Antiphonarium*.

The melodies for all these chants, which are to be found in the Vatican Edition, were written down from the tenth century, because had they not been written down they would have been forgotten, such was the ornateness of their melodies. Later on these melodies were pruned, and through the musical studies of the Benedictines of Solesmes in the *Paléographie Musicale* re-written from the manuscripts, and became the basis of Pius X's reforms. The results of these may be seen in the Vatican Edition. It is not my place to make any judgment on the value of this undertaking, but it is instructive to know that at an abbey such as the basilica of Maria Laach where great stress is laid on the singing of Gregorian Chant, the monastic choir does not sing the long involved melismatic chants of the Gradual during the Conventual Mass on ordinary week-days, but uses a psalm tone instead; only the Alleluia verse does the choir sing according to the melody to be found in the Vatican Edition. Here we have a typical case of 'excessive solemnity' (Alphons Beil), and that to such a degree that even in favourable circumstances it is found necessary to cut it down.

The three processional chants, four if we include the chants of the Gradual and Alleluia verse (today we describe them all as Proper chants), have remained through the centuries the musical climaxes of the Mass-liturgy.

In the age of Gothic art, when a taste for everything that appealed to the senses began to conquer, we find the beginnings of harmonised music. Previously there was no harmonised music, at least not in church, and when it did exist it was extremely primitive. It was usually an octave accompaniment of men's and boy's voices or an alternation between them, still customary in cathedrals today. Harmony was practically unknown, so that the greatest musical effect was obtained by the development and enrichment of the existing chant melodies. As harmonised music began to develop and feel its way into liturgical services, it was logical enough for it to make a start on the Proper chants. This was especially the case with the Gradual and Alleluia chants, and their melodies were soon accompanied by a second, third and even fourth voice. It was certainly a thankless task to compose and practise these Proper chants, as they could after all only be used once during the year. Later on, individual texts taken out of the Propers of the main feastdays were the only parts of the Proper to be sung in harmony; even today the offertory text is usually favoured in this way, e.g., *Terra tremuit*, *Reges Tharsis* and *Ave Maria*. It is also true of certain Propers which occur more frequently, as for example the Requiem Mass, where all four parts of the Proper are usually sung in harmony. But for the rest harmonised music was only a brief phase which was soon past.

It was soon found to be more convenient and more rewarding to compose harmonised settings of the Ordinary of the Mass: the *Kyrie*, *Gloria*, *Credo*, *Sanctus* and *Agnus Dei*.

How did this happen? The Ordinary consisted of texts which, as we have seen, belonged to the people; texts which from the earliest times had really been recited rather than sung. If that could be called 'singing', then also the public recitation of the Rosary could be called 'singing', because when people pray together in an orderly fashion one pitch is adopted and each sentence concludes with a cadence. We might say perhaps that the best example of this type of singing is the chanting of the Grace before meals in monastic communities. In any case during the Carolingian era the Ordinary of the Mass was not reckoned as belonging to the sung parts of the Mass, at least by musicians.

It is certainly a fact that even in the early Middle Ages the responses by the people as well as the singing of the Ordinary declined more and more. The responses by the people during the Carolingian era were still considered strongly desirable, and the *Sanctus* must have remained on the lips of the people for a long time. Even in the twelfth century there were still traces of this in our northern lands. But the liturgy of the Middle ages very soon became a monastic and a cathedral liturgy. Only in the monasteries were there still to be found men of considerable learning, but as far as the people were concerned the language became a barrier through which they could not break. In the monasteries and cathedrals on the other hand the numbers of monks and clergy increased; the enormous sanctuary in the plan of a Roman church is the best proof of this. The clergy seated in their choir-stalls were the chief performers of the liturgy. The clergy were at the same time the choir; the clergy and the choir were synonymous.

The clergy made up the choir and sang the Ordinary. Within the main body of the clergy was a group of the very best singers: this was the *Schola* and sang the Proper. The clergy of course were able to master the Proper much more easily than the people, especially in an artistic sense. Earlier there were separate melodies for the *Kyrie*, for the *Sanctus*, but no one setting for the whole Ordinary. These settings began to be composed from the thirteenth century, and the *Missa de Angelis* is the earliest example.

But the process did not stop there; the 'excessive solemnity' went on. From the fourteenth century men had begun to compose harmonised versions of the Ordinary in France. The new custom made slow headway, but in the sixteenth century it reigned supreme, at least in the large cities. The Ordinary now passed out of the hands of the clergy into the hands of specially trained singers, who could now be lay-people, and according to the practice of the Middle Ages were organised into guilds. But they were in fact lay-people and once again the question arose, where should they sing? This church choir could no longer sing in the sanctuary, with the result that it settled finally at the rear of the church, which we call nowadays the choir-loft, which also housed the by now highly developed organ. Again we see the development of a new branch of religious and ecclesiastical art: Church music now begins to reveal works of great artistic worth. We speak of the Viennese classics of Church music. The royal courts of the eighteenth and nineteenth centuries were the first to encourage this new art. This new form of liturgical celebration found its way everywhere, on a reduced scale, into the churches of town and country. It soon came to be regarded as an essential part of the celebration of the feast day. Soon this became true of Sundays, so that a harmonised Mass was said to be 'performed' with more or less pomp, just as a play or an opera is performed. What culture had gained, the people's worship had certainly lost. If we concede that on the great feast days of the Church the pomp and splendour of the music is a possible and even desirable way of expressing the spiritual joy felt on that feast day, and if we concede further that the hearing of a religious and artistic composition is also a means of religious edification, we must nevertheless deny that it should become the normal thing on Sundays. Because if the people are condemned absolutely to silence on account of a musical performance and grow accustomed to that silence, there ceases to exist a SOCIA EXSULTATIO, and in its place there is simply an *exsultatio* which has been cut off from the root of the community and condemned to wither away and die. But the evidence of a new and healthy consciousness grows, when today special groups of young people and parishes prefer to sing plain chant and straightforward hymns as opposed to the more artistic forms of musical culture.

A similar danger may be noted with regard to ceremonial and liturgical vestments. We can understand and even justify solemn and courtly ceremonies in, for example, a Pontifical High Mass, when the people desire to see the invisible expressed in visual form. We might mention here the carrying of lights and incense at the head of the papal procession; this stems directly from the court ceremonial of the Roman Emperor. From the same source derives the *sustentatio*, where two *diaconi honorarii* accompanied and originally supported the celebrant as he walked in procession; from the same source comes the *proskynesis*, the genuflection in front of the Bishop, as well as the pontifical sandals, the pallium and the Bishop's stole. But some of these ceremonies have been transferred from the papal and pontifical Masses to the ordinary priest's Mass, where they are to a degree less intelligible. The Solemn High Mass originated largely from the engrafting of episcopal ceremonies onto the priest's Mass, of which the authentic form is the *Missa cantata*.

The development of these ceremonies is connected with the fact that in the Roman liturgy (and similarly in other liturgies) the ceremonies occurring on great feast days and solemn functions would quite naturally be codified. Because at first they were the only ceremonies to be codified, they were the only ceremonies to be transferred from Rome to the Frankish dominions after the eighth century and provided the basis of the recently introduced Roman liturgy. For persons living in the Middle Ages accustomed to the feudal system and who were quite happy to contemplate scenes rather than listen and understand words, these forms may have been welcome. But the matter-of-fact, prosaic man of our own day has but little appreciation of such things.

We can at least be grateful to the royal courts for one custom, the value of which has not diminished with the passage of time; I refer to the use of candles and incense. It seems that candle-light was used quite early on not only for the entry of the Bishop, but also to accompany the Book of Gospels in the little procession before its solemn chant. The candlesticks

were placed near the altar, until about the year 1000 they
were placed actually on the altar. They serve as signs of
reverence towards the Mystery being enacted upon the
altar.

Less clear is the development of the use of incense. It has
various symbolical meanings. Incense burns before the
Blessed Sacrament (at the consecration and on other occasions). It is also used for the celebrant, apparently as a mark of
respect, but in reality as a sign and sacramental of purification
and dedication, just as it is similarly used for the people.

In the sphere of liturgical vestment I will mention only one
example which is, however, a typical illustration of the
dangers of embellishing already established forms. It is the
history of the chasuble.

The chasuble was originally, as is well known, a festive
cloak, the last survivor of ornamental dress towards the end of
the reign of the Roman Emperors. It was a sleeveless piece of
cloth completely surrounding the wearer. It has to be rucked
up in front in order to free the hands and this resulted in a
bundle of cloth in front. The early Middle Ages knew this
form of chasuble as the 'bell-tent'. Its entire decoration consisted of precious cloth, stitching and embroidery, which
emphasized the shape of the back and the lines of the shoulders.

In the Gothic period the cut was altered to some extent, and
the oval shape emphasized. A cross was embroidered on the
back, and this developed into a crucifix; figurate embroidery
was also added. The rear of the chasuble became a picture
gallery in miniature. The pictures were embroidered; this led
to the demand for smooth surfaces, the avoidance of creases
and the disappearance of any kind of sleeves altogether. Thus
appeared the Baroque chasuble, often richly decorated, but
its pair of stiff boards no longer have any claim to the title of
garment. The final product was the 'fiddleback', which
Clemens Hofbauer refused to recognize, but even today
in places has to be endured. The return of the so-called Gothic
chasuble in our time is a welcome sign that what is simple,
original and genuine can still be recognized.

We shall witness this kind of crisis again and again at very
different points in the liturgy. It is buried deep in the essence

of the Christian liturgy that on the one hand there exists the necessity to make religious worship as worthy, as beautiful and as rich as man is capable of doing (these are the forms of spiritual joy and exultation), while on the other hand at various points in history attempts are made to dispose of all surplus and unnecessary wealth and a return is sought to the living and fundamental forms.

We may perhaps see now that the poverty which now exists in certain countries may not be a misfortune, but possibly a blessing from God.

I conclude with an earnest plea that those priests who perform their sacred functions in such difficult circumstances may draw interior strength and grow in Faith and Love of Our Divine Lord, even though they lack the means for exterior decoration and development. May the *Socia exsultatio* of the spirits in Heaven find its worthy fulfilment especially in those priests.

THE END

The End

DATE DUE

GAYLORD			PRINTED IN U.S.A.